I0503570

HOW TO RETIRE RICH

Create the perfect retirement plan while you can

Justin Harrison

FOREWORD

W hen you think of retirement, the first thing that comes to mind is what we have been taught growing up which is to invest in a retirement fund.

We have been brainwashed by the media, schools and our parents to follow this route diligently and to trust the financial system, unfortunately, it doesn't work out that great for most people.

In this book, Justin gives you an entirely new perspective when it comes to retirement planning. Instead of trusting the government, he shows you how to design your own plan.

Instead of looking at the monetary value that you will be needing for retirement, he challenges you to determine the kind of lifestyle you would like to have first. Based on the lifestyle, he shows you how to calculate the amount you need.

Justin clearly shows you how to create a clear plan for your future, how to ensure that you retire with enough money to live your rich life and how to ensure that you never run out of money in your old age.

To not have a plan in place for your old age is like climbing into your car and driving without an end destination in sight. In this book, Justin guides you by the hand to ensure that you get clarity in terms of creating a bulletproof plan for your own retirement.

This information is essential for any individual, regardless of their age, to ensure that they retire comfortably, stress-free and to live a life of ultimate freedom during their old age.

It's extremely simple, easy to understand and you will have full confidence in yourself to design a plan that works for you instead of relying on government and financial advisors with your hard-earned money.

David Bester

TABLE OF CONTENTS

INTRODUCTION

A Canadian newspaper ran a story a few years back about an elderly man who was discovered huddled with his dog in his car, half-frozen to death. How did the man find himself in this predicament?

Turns out that through no fault of his own, he had simply run out of money. His wife had recently passed away after a two-year battle with cancer, and he had used the last of his savings to give her a dignified funeral. Now he could not find work, had lost his home and was trying to survive on help from his church and local non-profit organisations.

This may be an extreme example, but it exposes a dirty little secret about retirement planning. The secret is that often even the most forward-looking retirement plans don't fully protect against the risk of running out of money during retirement.

Investment firms and financial planners all promote their ability to create "worry-free" retirement plans. These plans are designed to produce retirement income by systematically "decumulating" the assets that the retiree had accumulated during working years.

Sometimes, there is even the insinuation that these plans will not only provide a retirement income but that the assets of the retiree may actually increase in value over the years.

The majority of these investment advisors are well-intentioned and do their best to create plans that will provide a comfortable retirement.

The problem is they rarely bring up the biggest risk that retirees face, and that is, what happens if the plan does not work as anticipated and the retiree runs out of money during retirement?

The reason banks, investment firms and financial planners seldom mention the risk of running out of money is because they lack the tools to guarantee that this hazard can be eliminated.

Nothing is crueller than having no more money in retirement, because when it happens, there are very few options available to rectify the situation.

Can you imagine how it would be to retire at 65, relying on a seemingly well-designed plan, only to discover at age 75 that your plan has run out of money?

What would your options be? Could you get back into the workforce? Become an Uber driver? How would you feel about becoming a burden on family or having to depend on charity simply to survive?

Fortunately, it is possible to design a retirement plan that can meet your income needs and at the same time guard against that risk.

No one product or approach will work on its own to achieve this objective, but a multifaceted plan is the best way to meet your retirement needs and protect against that risk.

As with all advice, I encourage you to keep an open mind and to always apply your logic when exploring these ideas.

STOP RELYING ON GOVERNMENT

I rrespective of your political ideology, there is one thing we can all agree on, and that is that no government is perfect.

In fact, if we look throughout history, including very recent history, governments have made a habit of failing its people at some point in time, and it has always affected the poor and the elderly first.

If you are in any way relying on your government for your retirement, you need to stop. So many people around the world are reliant in their old age on pensions, public health care, and worst of all they have all of their investments geographically limited to one government.

You need to start diversifying your plan today. I am not saying your government will fail, but I am saying there is a strong possibility they can, and if they do, you will be very glad that you did not rely entirely on your government to get you through your old age.

There is virtually not a single government around the world that has not at one point or another reduced its benefits for retirees, dipped into its citizen's pension funds, or worse yet had a few decades of economic instability causing retirees to have to make do with less.

Even if you save diligently, invest wisely and plan for your retirement in the traditional sense, chances are the one thing that can mess up your entire plan, is your government.

This is why you have to protect yourself from poor leadership, bad economic decisions, currency devaluations, trade disagreements and all the other stuff that's outside of your plan, and your control.

PENSION FUNDS
ARE BULLSHIT

P ension funds, social security, retirement annuities, retirement endowments, and other official retirement plans are all pretty much the same thing, just dressed up in a different way.

These are all forms of mandatory retirement savings and "force" people to set aside money for their retirement, and honestly, without it most people would not have the discipline to set the money aside.

So from the perspective that these forms of "forced" retirement savings plans ensure that the vast majority of people set aside money for their retirement and that they cannot access this money until they retire, it is actually a pretty good thing.

The problem, however, is that almost anytime people are either too lazy or lack the discipline to do things themselves, they surrender a huge amount of control to another entity in exchange for convenience, and such is the case with pension and retirement plans.

Let me first off say that having one of these plans is better than having nothing at all, but this is far from ideal.

If there is one thing I am absolutely certain of, every person wants to retire with as close to an ideal plan as possible, because the alternative is pretty scary.

So let's talk about traditional retirement plans

If you have a pension fund, social security, retirement annuity or retirement fund chances are you have all your eggs in one basket.

No matter how diversified your retirement portfolio is, if you have a traditional retirement plan, your entire pension is linked to your country of origin and that is the one thing that can unsettle your entire plan.

The single biggest disadvantage of these fixed pension plans is that you have in essence given up control of how and where your money is invested in exchange for the simplicity and discipline of someone else managing your money for you, and for having taken certain tax deductions along the way.

Don't be fooled however those tax deductions that incentivise you to save for your retirement, and that simplicity of having someone else manage your retirement fund, it comes with massive risk.

When things go wrong, they go horribly wrong. Just ask a citizen of a country that's been economically ruined by bad leadership. Countries like Zimbabwe and Venezuela are two extreme examples of this.

And if you think that won't happen in your backyard, consider that the world economic forum has reported as early as 2014 that the pension industry is already in such a deep financial crisis that it could well be the trigger for the largest global financial and economic meltdown ever seen.

This has largely been overlooked. Instead, it has been common to only discuss the pension industry in terms of the problems arising from ageing populations (which is of course also important and true).

While the recovery of many countries equity markets from the decline in 2007-09 may appear to look like good news for pension funds, it has not benefited the industry as much as you might expect.

Most pension funds moved away from equity investments over the last decade in their portfolios, increasing their share in bonds instead, and in so doing not only missed out on the high returns in the equity markets but ended up losing money in the bond markets. The net effect is that the pension industry in many countries is in a bad way.

According to a Citibank report from 2016, the 20 largest OECD countries alone have a US$78 trillion shortfall in funding pay-as-you-go and defined-benefit public pensions' obligations. This shortfall is far from trivial. **It is equivalent to about 1.8 times the value of these countries' collective national debt.**

Developed economies like Germany, Japan, and even the USA all have social security and pension plans that are on the brink of collapse because quite frankly they are not sustainable, they have been poorly managed and cannot possibly cater for retirees who are living longer.

And the cycle is only going to get worse because as retirement plans fail this generation of retirees will indirectly force the next generation to work longer, to retire with less causing the cycle the deepen.

And the problem is even worse if you are in a developing economy because many governments are forcing their pension funds to invest in prescribed assets, which is basically another way of saying that the state dictates that pensioners money will be used at preferential rates for the benefit of the state, such as funding state-owned enterprises.

In these developing economies pensioners savings is now seen as an alternative to getting loans from the International Monetary Fund (IMF), because these developing countries governments can dictate to the pension funds the rate at which they will loan them money, and these loans come with no conditions, unlike loans from the IMF.

And as for those pension plans that guarantee you a pension for life, good luck with that when the money runs out.

THE NO-BULLSHIT ALTERNATIVE

I f you already have a compulsory pension, then so be it, continue contributing to it and hope for the best, but at the same time start designing an alternative structure that mitigates risk, puts you in control and becomes your default plan going into retirement.

Designing your own retirement plan is about taking back control, it's about doing away with unnecessary fees, mitigating risk and most importantly ensuring you have income that will outlive you.

If your compulsory pension holds up, fantastic, you will have two pension plans making sure you have a comfortable and most importantly independent retirement. If not, you will be very glad you started a second plan and that you thought ahead.

The benefits of creating your own pension plan:

- You are not limited to any specific investment category, and you can choose to put your money anywhere in the market.

- You can invest outside of your own country to diversify in multiple currencies to reduce your risk.

- You can avoid hefty long term management fees, which in turn will increase the overall value of your portfolio.

- You will have the control to quickly move your money in and out of investments and markets as you see fit.

- You have the ability to spread your money around through various investments and greatly reduce your overall risk.

- You don't have to wait until you reach a specific age to be able to access the benefits of your pension.

- You have a far greater chance of exponentially growing your capital and your income.

- No government can attach your pension savings if you have invested and diversified wisely.

The negative side of creating your own pension plan:

- It requires patience, persistence and most importantly a lot of self-discipline over a long period of time.

- You have to be committed to consistently putting away part of your income and be prepared not to touch it.

- You have to be committed to actively managing your money and taking a hands-on approach to growing your funds.

Investment Options:

There literally is no limit to the investment options when you start to design your own retirement fund, what is important is that you set money aside every month from your income and that you begin to invest that into vehicles that are relatively safe.

These investments should generate returns that not only beat inflation but should also give you the benefit of compound interest over the period that you are contributing and not drawing from "your personal pension fund".

Later when you do retire, you should still aim to draw less than the full amount earned by your "personal pension fund", to ensure that the fund continues to grow and therefore outlives you.

Here are some ideas for your "personal pension fund":

- **FIXED TERM SAVINGS:** such money market accounts, retail bond investments, fixed deposits etc.

- **STOCK MARKET:** blue-chip stocks, index funds, mutual funds or individual stocks with high yielding dividends.

- **REAL ESTATE:** Property funds, or rental property that you either manage yourself or have managed on your behalf.

- **ALTERNATIVE STRUCTURED INVEST-MENTS:** Hedge funds, private equity funds, or other guaranteed structured products.

- **ALTERNATIVE UNSTRUCTURED INVEST-MENTS:** Small business or shares in a small business, peer to peer lending etc.

This is by no means a comprehensive list, however, it is a very good starting point when you are looking for places to invest your money.

If you have not already done so I highly suggest you get yourself a copy of my other two books compound interest secrets and stock investing secrets

The biggest key to a secure personal retirement

fund is to spread your money around. In other words, don't put all your eggs in one basket.

Instead, focus on diversity in your portfolio, and spread your investments across asset classes, through different currencies and across different countries. This will give you long term stability.

LIFESTYLE PLANNING FOR RETIREMENT

T he best advice you will get from this book is to plan for your retirement based on lifestyle, not current income.

There's a rule of thumb that says you should budget a certain percentage of your income towards retirement. Many experts say you should set aside 10 to 15 percent of your income for your golden years.

However I would suggest a competing theory, and that is that you should budget for retirement based on the lifestyle you plan to enjoy, not the income that you currently earn. Everyone's ideal lifestyle in retirement is different, and traditional retirement advice is misleading.

For example, in retirement you may be content with living simply, cooking your own meals, cleaning your own home, and spending your time playing with your grandkids. If that's your ideal lifestyle you don't necessarily need to budget 15 percent of your after-tax income towards retirement unless you start saving later in life.

On the other hand, if you want the excitement of sailing around the world, or playing golf weekly, taking art lessons and travelling to a beachside villa regularly, you'll probably need to budget more than 15 percent towards retirement to achieve those goals.

In fact, when most people start to plan their ideal retirement lifestyle, they start to realize they want far less than they originally imagined, and this is the reason younger financially savvy people are re-tiring early these days. They simply find passive income streams that will allow them to live their ideal retired lifestyle now.

There are eight keys that you should think about as you create this picture of your retirement life. This will give you a structure and foundation to build your plans.

1. Having a positive attitude towards your future

Sociologists have identified at least six separate "life transitions" that will affect most people as they move through their retirement life. Perhaps the greatest transition of all is the one that you see each time you look in a mirror and see yourself change. It is easy to forget that "getting older" is a physical issue, not a mental one.

Plan ahead to surround yourself with positivity, and increase your ability to 'roll with the punches' as life begins to throw the ageing process at you.

2. Have a clear vision of the kind of life that you want

Far too many people make the mistake of thinking that the financial plan and the retirement plan are the same thing and that the life part will take care of itself.

This stage of your life deserves a more holistic look and plan than simply assuming that you are beginning a thirty-year long weekend.

What do you want your life to look like? What changes do you anticipate along the way? How will you get the most out of each and every day? Those are important questions as you contemplate your move into this next phase of your life.

3. Have a healthy approach to mental and physical ageing

While the ageing process affects us all in different ways, there are some things that we can all do to ensure that we "put time on our side". Most people think that being healthy physically is the key to healthy ageing.

In retirement, healthy mental ageing is just as important, if not more so. Make sure you have a plan to do something each and every day to nourish your need to use and expand your mind in retirement.

4. Have a positive definition of 'work'

Your work is the thing that you do to contribute your skills, experience, labour or knowledge to society in some way. It is also a way for you to "self-actualize" and create positive stress in your life. Even when you leave the workplace, you will still have a need to share your workplace strengths and transferable skills. Many retirees use volunteering as a way to replace the things that they miss most about their previous work and as a way to continue to contribute and "self-actualize".

5. Nurture family and personal relationships

Our close personal relationships define us, give us a purpose for living our lives and encourage us to create life goals. Psychologists have identified our desire to share ourselves as a basic human need, and researchers have found that people in satisfying personal relationships have fewer illnesses.

In real-life terms, having people close to you who will share your life and be there for you will not only add to your overall life enjoyment but will also add years to your life!

6. Have an active social network

Successful retirees generally have robust social networks that provide them with friendship, fulfilling activities and life structure. As part of your retirement plan, you might want to think about the quality of the social network that you have today and your plans to build it.

One of the lessons that we can learn about the ageing process is that our social networks begin to shrink, especially if we aren't continually adding to them, and so it makes good sense to continue to seek out new opportunities to socialize and make new friends all the time.

7. Have a balanced approach to leisure

Leisure is a fundamental human need. We use it to recharge our batteries, to act as a diversion in our lives, to create excitement, anticipation or simply to rest and contemplate. Things change, however, when leisure becomes the central focus of our lives.

Leisure, by its very nature, loses its lustre when it is the norm in our life rather than the diversion. For many retirees, the idea of leisure is associated with "not having to do anything." In the end, a lack of stimulation affects our mental and emotional state and then ultimately our physical well being. Successful retirees balance their leisure over many different activities and take the opportunity to do new things.

8. Maintaining 'financial comfort'

Some retirees feel that a happy retirement is guaranteed by financial security. However, there is no price tag on a successful retirement. As someone once said, "having a million dollars is NOT a retirement plan!" Financial comfort refers to being able to manage your life in a satisfying and fulfilling way using the financial resources that you have.

If financial discomfort contributes to retirement stress, then your financial plan becomes a negative rather than a positive. The keys to achieving financial comfort are to have a clear understanding of the financial resources you have and the demands on your money that will come from the life you lead.

HEALTH PLANNING FOR RETIREMENT

T he cost of healthcare is an important consideration when planning for retirement. Health care is the largest type of expense people face heading into retirement, which is why planning for your health in retirement is essential to ensure you don't drain your funds.

We have all seen it happen. A good friend, family member, or someone we work with finally reaches his retirement day and drops dead seemingly almost as soon as he retired, or worse yet becomes frail almost the day after they retire start ageing rapidly.

I have mentioned this as in the lifestyle planning section, but I will mention it again here as part of the health planning for retirement section as well because I believe this is so important it deserves a second mention, if not a dedicated section within this course

The single most important part of planning for your health in retirement is not the financial aspect or access to medical facilities, but rather the life-style you plan to lead in retirement.

It is critical to your good health that you remain physically and mentally active, that you dedicate yourself in retirement, not to a life of total leisure, but a life of purpose and balance. This will ensure good health and less pressure ultimately on your finances.

I am by no means suggesting you should ignore the financial aspects of your health or the logistical aspects either, however, I am suggesting that you take a more holistic approach to your health and fix the problems before they occur.

With that said here are a few financial and logistical considerations to take into account when heading into retirement:

- Plan around single-story living, or if you live in an apartment, make sure there is easy wheelchair easy. Don't wait until you need this to make the changes.

- Try to live close to public transport routes so that when the time comes where you cannot drive, or choose not to, you can still be mobile and move around.

- Try to live within a reasonable distance of good doctors, dentists, hospitals and other health providers.

- Compare senior/retiree medical plans before heading into retirement. Find the one that works for you and your budget and then try to get onto that plan sooner rather than later.

- Plan your living environment around your planned social activities to ensure your golden years are not spent in isolation.

Additional health planning tips:

- Plan to make daily exercise in retirement part of your routine, but instead of going to the gym, live in an environment where you can walk to the shops, or the park etc. This

way your commute becomes your exercise
routine.

- Plan to have a schedule and a structure in
retirement. Studies have shown that retirees
who structure their time live healthier hap-
pier lives and are less prone to illness.

- Plan your retirement around your ideal
location. If you want to be in the mountains or
perhaps the beach, go there. Being where you
are happiest will ensure good health.

- Plan to avoid depression and isolation.
Ensure you are actively surrounded by friends
and family on a regular basis.

- Plan for health setbacks know they might
happen and if they do keep a positive attitude
to overcome them.

- Plan to own and care for a dog in retirement.
Multiple studies have shown that retired dog
owners need fewer doctor visits have lower
cholesterol, lower blood pressure and a lower
heart attack risk than people without dogs.

- Plan to continue to think of yourself as young. Multiple studies have found that your mental attitude can reverse the effects of ageing and improve physical health.

- Plan to socialize with people younger than you. This will keep you active and ensure that a sense of purpose.

FINANCIAL PLANNING FOR RETIREMENT

P lanning financially for your retirement is actually much easier than you would expect. The difficult part is having the commitment to sticking with the plan all the way through until retirement.

Again I will refer back to the lifestyle planning section before we jump into the financial aspects here and remind you that before you start calculating numbers, you should ideally be looking at the lifestyle plan first so you can estimate how much money you will be needing.

As you plan for how much money you'll need in retirement, there are two popular rules of thumb that can outline the answer for you.

Multiply By 25 Rule:

The Multiply by 25 Rule estimates how much money you'll need invested in your retirement fund by multiplying your desired annual income by 25.

For example, if you want an income of $40,000 per year, you will need $1 million dollars invested in your retirement portfolio. ($40,000 x 25 equals $1 million.) If you want an income of $50,000 per year, you need $1.25 million invested, and so on.

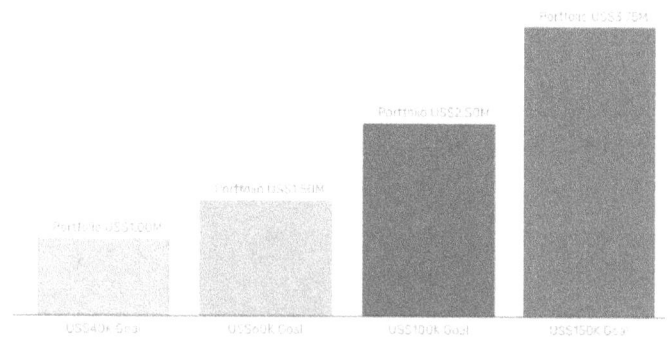

This rule of thumb estimates the amount of income that you can withdraw from your investment port-folio without touching the capital amount in your portfolio and assuming you will be able to generate an annualized real return in excess of 4 percent per year.

The 4 Percent Rule:

The 4 Percent Rule, guides how much money you can withdraw annually once you're retired, without cutting into your investment principal amount (capital).

As the name suggests, this rule of thumb says you should only withdraw 4 percent of your retirement portfolio annually.

For example, let's say you retire with $700,000 in your portfolio. In your first year of retirement, you can safely withdraw $28,000. ($700,000 x 0.04 equals $28,000.) and so on.

Income VS Capital:

One final consideration when you are doing your financial planning is to take into account that you may well be able to achieve your desired income goals with considerably less capital, depending on the income you are able to generate from the assets you invest into.

It is or this reason that many people looking to retire early plan to set up a small business or provide services that can provide them with a passive income stream that will provide a higher return than normal investment vehicles in addition to their investment portfolio.

Property for example can often generate a much higher return, especially if you run an Airbnb, or provide student accommodation.

There are also a number of small businesses that can generate passive income streams that could provide supplemental income and would, therefore, lower the amount of capital you would need invested in order to generate the return you need to meet your income goals.

When you are doing your financial planning take these elements into account, and think carefully if you are going to rely purely on investing your money or if you are going to still actively participate (all be it passively) in the marketplace for additional returns.

WHAT'S YOUR NUMBER

Most people think in terms of their retirement goal as either an age by which they want to retire or how much they want to retire with in the bank. I however would like to pose an alternative option for you.

I would like you to think about your retirement in terms of lifestyle, then sit and draw up a realistic budget after having done some thorough homework on the costs of such a lifestyle.

Everyone is different, everyone is unique and so there are no rules here. This is about taking a blank sheet of paper and creating your ideal lifestyle and figuring out what it's going to cost to live that lifestyle every month.

Once you know that number, write it down. That's the first important number in your retirement plan. Next, multiply that number by 25 and the answer is your retirement number.

Congratulations, you now have a realistic goal, you now have an actual workable and sustainable retirement plan and you can get working towards that goal. It's amazing what that kind of clarity will bring to your retirement planning.

Such clarity in fact that an entire generation of millennials have managed to retire by the age of 30 because they realized, all you need to retire is a financial plan that sets you free from having to "work" for your money. That's all that retirement actually is.

So what's your number?

Make a list of all the expenses you anticipate you will incur monthly when you retire. Don't worry too much about inflation right now, because you'll only be drawing 4% of your invested income so your portfolio will grow to take care of inflation in real terms.

Once you have a monthly budget, multiply that by 12 to get an annual budget amount. Then multiply your annual budget by 25 to get to the capital amount you need invested before you can retire comfortably.

HOUSING	$ 1,300.00
TRANSPORTATION	$ 800.00
HEALTH CARE	$ 500.00
INSURANCE	$ 300.00
CASH	$ 500.00
ENTERTAINMENT	$ 500.00
TRAVEL	$ 500.00
GROCERIES	$ 800.00
EATING OUT	$ 250.00
MEMBERSHIPS	$ 500.00
CLOTHING	$ 200.00
COMMUNICATIONS	$ 300.00
GIFTS	$ 200.00
SUNDRY	$ 500.00
CABLE TV	$ 100.00
OTHER MEDICAL	$ 500.00
HOBBIES	$ 250.00
TOTAL MONTHLY	**$ 8,000.00**
TOTAL ANNUAL	**$ 96,000.00**
RETIREMENT NUMBER	**$ 2,400,000.00**

CLOSING THOUGHTS

M any people think about retirement as a destination, and get bogged down in the financial details. I hope that this book inspires you to look at how to retire rich from a new perspective because retiring rich is about more than money, **it's about lifestyle design.**

In closing, I would like to share with you a Mexican fishing parable shared with me a few years ago while I was living in Mexico. This story resonated with me, and I hope it inspires you to reassess how you live your life and to rethink your retirement plans.

The Mexican Fisherman

An American investment banker was taking a much-needed vacation in a small coastal Mexican village when a small boat with just one fisherman docked. The boat had several large, fresh fish in it.

The investment banker was impressed by the quality of the fish and asked the Mexican how long it took to catch them. The Mexican replied, "Only a little while." The banker then asked why he didn't stay out longer and catch more fish?

The Mexican fisherman replied he had enough to support his family's immediate needs. The American then asked, "But what do you do with the rest of your time?"

The Mexican fisherman replied, "I sleep late, fish a little, play with my children, take siesta with my wife, stroll into the village each evening where I sip wine and play guitar with my amigos: I have a full and busy life, señor."

The investment banker scoffed, "I am an Ivy League MBA, and I could help you. You could spend more time fishing and with the proceeds buy a bigger boat, and with the proceeds from the bigger boat, you could buy several boats until eventually, you would have a whole fleet of fishing boats. Instead of selling your catch to the middleman you could sell directly to the processor, eventually opening your own cannery. You could control the product, processing and distribution."

Then he added, "Of course, you would need to leave this small coastal fishing village and move to Mexico City where you would run your growing enterprise."

The Mexican fisherman asked, "But señor, how long will this all take?" To which the American replied, "15-20 years."

"But what then?" asked the Mexican.

The American laughed and said, "That's the best part. When the time is right you would announce an IPO and sell your company stock to the public and become very rich. You could make millions."

"Millions, señor? Then what?"

To which the investment banker replied, "Then you would retire. You could move to a small coastal fishing village where you would sleep late, fish a little, play with your kids, take siesta with your wife, stroll to the village in the evenings where you could sip wine and play your guitar with your amigos."

ACKNOWLEDGEMENTS

I would like to thank my business partners, Dale Maxwell, Laura Palmeri, David Bester and Chris du Toit who have held down the fort while I took the time to write this book. Without their support and input, this book would never have become a reality.

I would especially like to thank Laura for her critical eye and constant proofreading, which helps a dyslexic, barely literate guy like myself seem capable of writing something worth reading.

I would also like to extend an extra-special thank you to my wife Andrea who as always offers constant constructive criticism and input, and unwavering support. Thank you for always making sure I have no distractions when I write and for your total commitment. I could not have asked for a better partner.

Last but not least, I would like to give an extra heartfelt thank you to David for sharing my vision and helping bring these ideas to life. Your work ethic and dedication to Global Money Academy is inspiring.

First printing, 2019.

Team 6 Investment Holdings Ltd.
5th Floor, Ritter House,
Wickhams Clay II,
Road Town, Tortola
British Virgin Islands

www.globalmoneyacademy.com